the best GIFT EVER

Written by
Dr. Daniela Owen

Illustrated by
Gülce Baycik

About the Author

Dr. Daniela Owen is a psychologist who brings to life healthy mind concepts and strategies for children everywhere. For more about the author please check out

drdanielaowen.com

For Lila & Maxwell, my best gifts ever.

For all inquiries, please contact us at:
info@drdanielaowen.com

To see more of our books, visit us at:
www.drdanielaowen.com

THIS BOOK IS
GIVEN WITH LOVE TO...

_____

The best gift ever
doesn't come from boxes in a row.

It doesn't come pretty,
tied up in a bow.

It doesn't come in tissue paper
tucked into a bag.

Wishing You Happy Holidays! ~ ENJOY!

It doesn't come with messages
written on a tag.

The best gift ever
won't be too boring or small.

Items	Quantity

Cute Dino Plush

1

Stacking Stick

1

Hot Air Balloon Toy

1

Colorful Ball

1

It isn't something that's
bought online or at the mall.

The best gift ever isn't something you can touch, taste, or see.

You can't buy it with money
because it is free!

The best gift ever isn't farmed,
and it doesn't grow on a tree.

It isn't made in an office
or in a factory.

The best gift ever
isn't pulled from a magic top hat.

It isn't baked in an oven
or rolled out on a mat.

The best gift ever isn't something that you can eat or use.

The best gift ever isn't something
that you can break or lose.

The best gift ever comes in all colors, shapes, and sizes.

It's found around the world,
on farms and in high rises.

You can share the best gift ever with a furry friend.

It doesn't have to stay at home.
It's something you can send.

The best gift ever forms a
connection between you and me.

It makes us feel warm,
all safe and cuddly.

The best gift ever makes us
sing, smile, laugh, and "coo".

The best gift ever is unlimited...
it's made inside of you.

The best gift ever is

LOVE

shared between family and friends.

The best part of the best gift ever...
is that it never ends!